Hi, I'm **Carrie.**

And I'm **David.**

Welcome to our **JUMP UP** and **JOIN IN** series.

We hope you enjoy reading the books and joining in with the songs.

This book is called **Lion's Speedy Sauce.**

I love this one, it's about **rhythm** and counting.

Yeah, it's a good one. Remember to **turn the page** when you hear this sound . . .

ROAR!

First American Edition 2013
Kane Miller, A Division of EDC Publishing

Text copyright © Carrie and David Grant 2013
Illustrations copyright © Ailie Busby 2013

First published in Great Britain in 2013 by Egmont UK Limited

For information contact:
Kane Miller, A Division of EDC Publishing
P.O. Box 470663
Tulsa, OK 74147-0663
www.kanemiller.com
www.edcpub.com

Library of Congress Control Number: 2012956107

Printed in China
1 2 3 4 5 6 7 8 9 10
ISBN: 978-1-61067-180-4

Please note:
Adult supervision is recommended when
scissors are in use.

For
Olivia, Talia,
Imogen and Nathan
– Carrie and David –

For Ruby x
– Ailie –

Carrie and David Grant

Lion's Speedy Sauce

Illustrations by Ailie Busby

Remember to turn the page
when the lion **roars!**

Kane Miller
A DIVISION OF EDC PUBLISHING

Lion's band
was practicing for
an important concert
at the Summer Fair.

He kept time with the bongos.

"One, two, one, two!"

But the sun was shining so brightly that Lion began to feel a little bit sleepy . . .

"One . . .

two . . .

And the band began to march s l o w e r . . .

and slower...

and slower...

The band decided to buy Lion
a clock to help him
keep time . . .

tick-tock

tick-tock

to lion

but the tick-tock, tick-tock
seemed to make Lion even sleepier!

"Phew," gasped the band, who had almost fallen asleep too.

Lunch
was Lion's
favorite
curry!

. . . the band added a little bit more!

After such a spicy lunch Lion felt wide awake.
He beat his bongos **in time**.

"One, two,

one,

two!"

The band marched into town
to play at the Summer Fair
and thanks to Lion's spicy,
speedy sauce . . .

. . . they were a **roaring** success!

Lion's Speedy Sauce sing-along song

Attention!

It's really a waste,
We're losing the race,
My marching band
Can't find the pace.
I say to go slow,
I say to go quick,
My speedy sauce might do the trick
(here we go).

Chorus:
Left, right, left, right, keep the pace,
Marching up and down
(come on, come on).
Left, right, left, right, our parade
Is marching into town.

Look sharp.
Hey!
Come on.
That's better.

Can this really be,
That suddenly
My soldiers march along with me.
I say to go slow,
I say to go quick,
My speedy sauce has done the trick
(come on now).

Chorus:
Left, right, left, right, keep the pace,
Marching up and down
(you're looking good now).
Left, right, left, right, our parade
Is marching into town (step it up x 4).

Woo!
Come on.
Are you ready?
All together now!

Left, right, left, right,
Keep it up, keep it up.
Left, right, left, right,
Speed it up, speed it up.
Left, right, left, right,
Keep it up, keep it up.
Left, right, left, right,
Come on, let's go!

Oh oh oh, oh oh oh, oh oh oh, oh,
Keep it going now.
Oh oh oh, oh oh oh, oh oh oh, oh,
Keep it up, keep it up, keep it up.

Chorus:
Left, right, left, right, keep the pace,
Marching up and down.
(Boom, boom, boom, boom, boom!)
Left, right, left, right, our parade
Is marching into town.

Oh oh oh, oh oh oh, oh oh oh, oh,
Look left, look right.
Oh oh oh (come on), oh oh oh (come on),
oh oh oh, oh,
Keep it up, keep it up, keep it up now.

Chorus x 3

Attention!

When you play Track **7**, the karaoke track, sing along
to the whole song! Your special solo parts are in **bold**.

Clever Clapping on the Beat

This story was all about **rhythm**.

Rhythm helps music to flow and keeping **in time** is a great thing to practice.

Count from **1** to **4** over and over, like this:

1   2   3   4   1   2   3   4

Now try **clapping** every time you say **1** and **3**, like this:

1   2   **3**   4   **1**   2   **3**   4

Now you can swap numbers and clap every time you say **2** and **4**, like this:

1 **2** 3 **4** 1 **2** 3 **4**

Now, if there are **two** of you, one can clap on the **1** and **3** and the other on the **2** and **4**, like this:

1 **2** **3** **4** **1** **2** **3** **4**

For our **Jump Up and Join In** series we really want to get children interested in music and how it works. It shouldn't have to be rocket science and we want to encourage you as a parent, teacher or caregiver to teach your children with confidence. If **you** can learn it then **you** can pass it on.

Track 6 Super Scales on the Stairs

In this book we're going to start with **scales**. Look at the picture of the stairs. Let's think about our voices climbing up the stairs . . .

4
(Fa)

3
(Mi)

lowest

2
(Re)

1
(Do)

Make your own Bangin' Bongos!

You'll need:

Two saucepans*   Wax paper   Big rubber bands
Tape   Wide ribbon   Pencil   Scissors

* You can also make the bongos with flowerpots or empty trash cans.

Step 1 Put the saucepans upside down on top of the wax paper. Draw around the rims of both pans with a pencil.

Cut out two big circles, slightly bigger than the pencil circles you have just drawn.

Step 2 Attach a circle around the rim of each saucepan with the rubber bands and secure with tape.

Make sure the paper is pulled very tightly around the rim of each pan.

Step 4 Now bang those bongos and keep a steady beat, just like Lion!

Step 3 Wrap the wide ribbon underneath the rim of each saucepan to cover up the rubber band and the tape.

Tie in a bow around the handle.

About Carrie and David

England's Carrie and David are best known for their hugely successful UK CBeebies series, *Carrie and David's Popshop*. They have coached Take That, The Saturdays and The Spice Girls and have a top-selling vocal coaching book and DVD. In 2008 they were awarded a BASCA for their lifetime services to the music industry.

Parents to four children, Carrie and David are passionate about getting all children to sing and are keen to encourage adults to feel more confident in teaching their little ones music skills from an early age. The *Jump Up and Join In* series was born as a result of this passion and will help young children learn a set of basic skills and develop a real love of music. As ambassadors for Sing Up – a not-for-profit organization providing the complete singing solution for schools in Britain – and judges of the young singers on BBC 1's Comic Relief Does Glee Club, Carrie and David believe children everywhere should be given the tools to enjoy, and to feel confident about, practicing music in all its shapes and forms.

Thanks for jumping up
and joining in!
Till the next time, bye!